EASY CARPENTRY PROJECTS FOR CHILDREN

EASY CARPENTRY

PROJECTS FOR CHILDREN

by Jerome E. Leavitt

Illustrated by Margrete Cunningham

DOVER PUBLICATIONS, INC., New York

This Dover edition, first published in 1986, is an unabridged and slightly
corrected republication of the work originally published by Sterling Publishing Co., Inc., New York, in 1959, under the title *Carpentry for Children*.
The present edition is published by special arrangement with Sterling
Publishing Co., Inc., Two Park Avenue, New York, N.Y. 10016.

Library of Congress Cataloging-in-Publication Data

Leavitt, Jerome Edward, 1916–
  Easy carpentry projects for children.

  Reprint. Originally published: Carpentry for children. New York : Sterling Pub. Co., 1959.
  Summary: Instructions for making fifteen different articles from wood,
with information on materials and tools and general directions for any
woodworking project.
  1. Woodwork—Juvenile literature. 2. Carpentry—Juvenile literature.
[1. Woodwork. 2. Carpentry] I. Title.
TT185.L4 1986   684'.08   85-20645
  ISBN-13: 978-0-486-25057-1 (pbk.)
  ISBN-10: 0-486-25057-1 (pbk.)

Manufactured in the United States by Courier Corporation
25057115
www.doverpublications.com

PREFACE

This book, written especially for boys and girls, gives directions for making fifteen different articles out of wood. It tells you about the materials to use and the best way to use tools to make the articles. The last two sections, "Steps in Squaring a Block of Wood," and "Steps in Wood Finishing" give general directions that apply to all woodworking projects. Therefore, it is a good idea to read these chapters before you start to work on any of the projects. It is assumed that the young carpenter has access to a home or school shop with a workbench and a vise.

Before you start to build any of the projects read the complete directions carefully and study the illustrations. If you collect all the necessary materials and tools before you start, it will be much easier for you to follow the directions step by step.

The author wishes to thank the editor and publishers of *Junior Arts and Activities* for permission to use some of these ideas that formerly appeared in that publication.

JEROME E. LEAVITT

CONTENTS

TOOLS FOR A JUNIOR WOODWORKER'S WORKSHOP

Different articles require different tools in their construction. This is a list of tools that you will need for many but not all of the projects in this book.

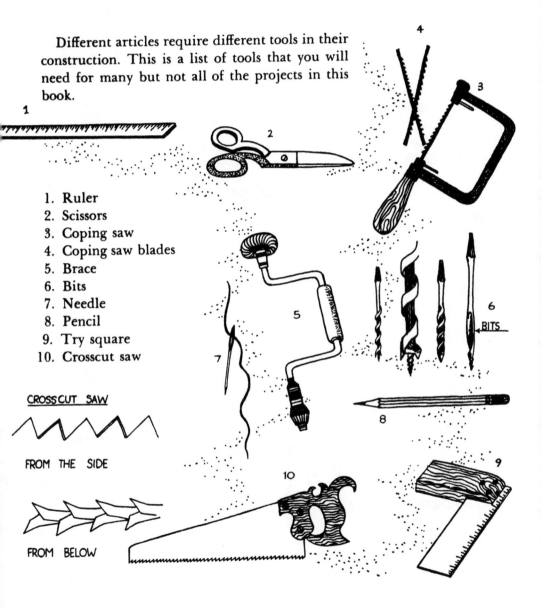

1. Ruler
2. Scissors
3. Coping saw
4. Coping saw blades
5. Brace
6. Bits
7. Needle
8. Pencil
9. Try square
10. Crosscut saw

CROSSCUT SAW

FROM THE SIDE

FROM BELOW

BITS

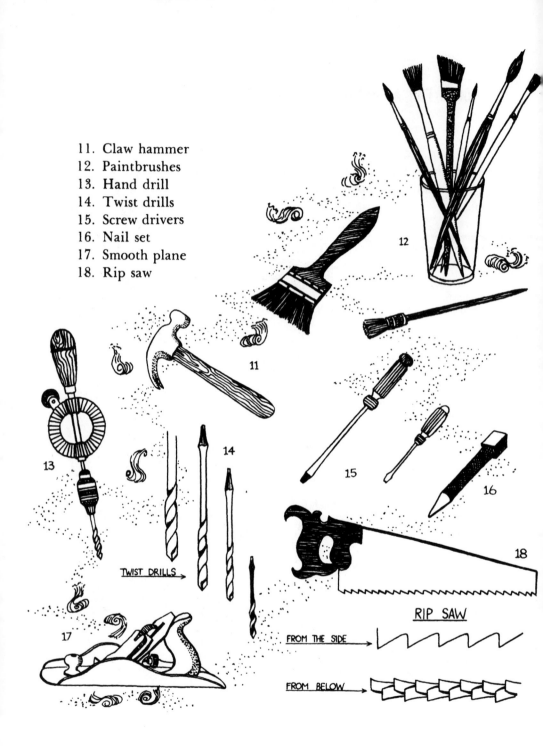

11. Claw hammer
12. Paintbrushes
13. Hand drill
14. Twist drills
15. Screw drivers
16. Nail set
17. Smooth plane
18. Rip saw

TWIST DRILLS

RIP SAW

FROM THE SIDE

FROM BELOW

1. SAILBOAT

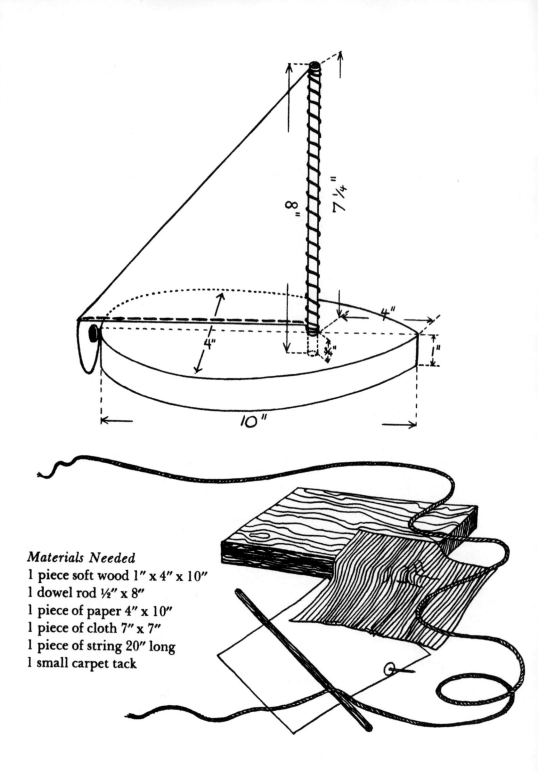

8"

7¼"

4"

4"

¼"

10"

1"

Materials Needed
1 piece soft wood 1" x 4" x 10"
1 dowel rod ½" x 8"
1 piece of paper 4" x 10"
1 piece of cloth 7" x 7"
1 piece of string 20" long
1 small carpet tack

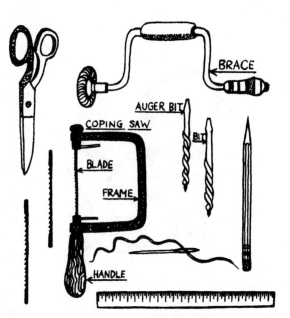

Tools Needed
1 ruler
1 pair of scissors
1 coping saw
3 coping saw blades
1 brace
1 auger bit
1½″ bit
1 needle with large eye
1 pencil

You can make a simple sailboat from a piece of soft wood, such as pine, fir, or cypress. Make the mast from a dowel rod (a round stick) of birch or maple.

Before you begin to work, prepare all the necessary tools and materials listed above.

The first step is to make a pattern of the deck. Cut a piece of paper 4 inches wide and 10 inches long. Then draw the deck shape (as shown) on the paper and cut it out. After this, fold the pattern the long way down the middle and trim it to make it even.

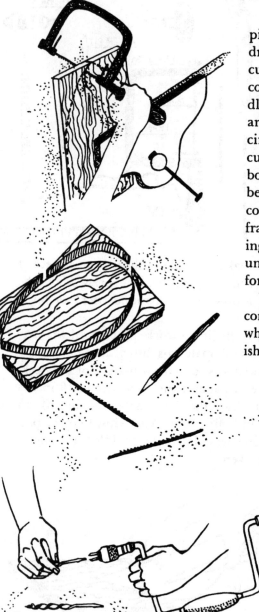

Now place the pattern on your piece of 1-inch-thick, soft wood and draw the outline of the deck. Next, cut it out with a coping saw. (A coping saw is made of a frame, handle, and blade. Because the blades are thin they can be used to cut circles and curved lines.) When you cut out the boat deck, fasten the board in the vise on your workbench and have the teeth of the coping saw point away from the frame. To make a turn when sawing, saw back and forth at one spot until you cut a fairly wide groove for the blade to turn in.

When you have the deck outline completely sawed you also have the whole bottom of the boat. To finish it off, you might like to whittle the bottom edge with a pocketknife until it is rounded the way a real boat is.

For the mast, drill a ½-inch round hole in the deck, 4 inches from the point (bow) and on the center line of the boat. Use a brace to hold this drill, which is called an auger bit. Auger bits are only used on wood because they are not strong enough to cut metal. To put the bit into the brace, open the jaws, slide in the bit, and tighten it. To use it, hold the brace near the bit with your left hand, place the knob against your body, and grasp the handle with your right hand. Then push the screw of the bit into the wood and turn the handle clockwise. Drill the hole only ¾-inch deep. Don't go through the 1-inch deck wood.

Make your mast 8 inches long, cutting it from a ½-inch-thick dowel rod. Push the mast into the hole you have prepared.

Make your sail by folding a 7-inch-square piece of cloth in half diagonally, so it forms a triangle. Then cut on the fold. Only one of these triangles is needed for the sail. Tie one end of your string to the top of the mast and thread the large-eyed needle with the string. Sew the sail on the mast by drawing the needle through the sail and around the mast from top to bottom. Then tie the string around the bottom of the mast and sew it through the bottom of the sail, allowing about 6 inches to extend beyond the sail. (See illustration on page 14.) Now tie the loose end of the string to a tack placed in the center of the back (stern) edge of the boat.

Your boat is now ready to be tried out in the water.

2. BIRD FEEDER

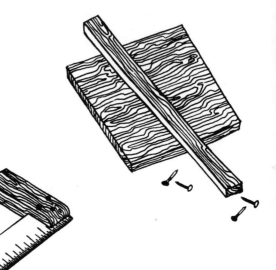

Materials Needed
1 piece of wood ½″ x 10″ x 10″
1 piece of wood ½″ x 2″ x 23″
16 1¼″ (3d) common nails
1 small can of linseed oil or stain

Tools Needed
1 try square
1 crosscut saw
1 hammer
1 paintbrush
1 pencil

For cold weather fun, you might like to make an open bird feeder to attract the winter birds to your yard. You can make this bird feeder from a few pieces of scrap wood such as are often found around the house.

First assemble the tools and materials listed above.

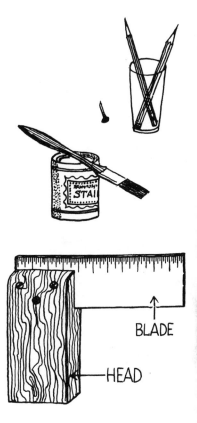

Cut the 10-inch bottom for the feeder from a board ½-inch thick by 10 inches wide. This is done by measuring 10 inches from a good straight end of the board. Then draw a line across the board, using a try square to guide your pencil. (A try square is a measuring tool made up of a head and blade fastened together at right angles. The blade is also used as a ruler.) When you draw the line, hold the head of the square firmly against the edge of the board while the blade of the square just touches your 10-inch mark.

Place the board now in your vise and cut it on the line with a crosscut saw. A crosscut saw is the most common of the hand saws and is used for cutting across the grain of a piece of wood. When

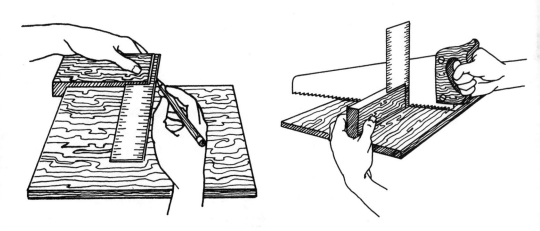

CROSSCUT SAW

FROM THE SIDE

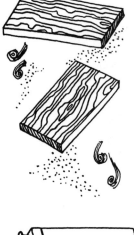

FROM BELOW

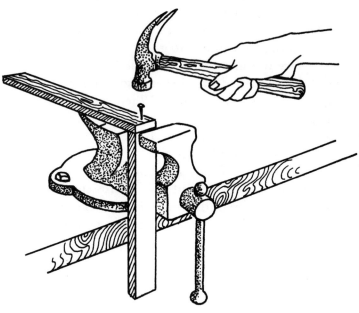

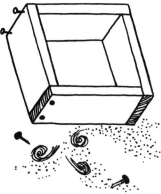

you saw, hold the saw firmly, and guide it with your right hand. Hold the board with your left hand. Notice how the teeth scratch out a path

before they cut out small chips. When you have your piece of wood just about sawed off, saw slowly and easily so you do not split the small piece of wood remaining to be cut off.

You make the frame with four 5¾-inch side pieces cut from a board ½-inch thick, 2 inches wide and 23 inches long. Measure and mark the four side pieces with the try square and cut off with the crosscut saw in the same way as for the bottom piece.

To assemble the bird feeder, you first nail the side pieces together at each joint with two 1¼-inch wire nails. Wire nails are nails with heads. Nailing the pieces together will be easy if you secure one piece in a vice. Then nail one side of it to the end of another, as shown in the illustration. Be sure that you nail *one* side of each board to an *end* of another board, as shown. Repeat this until all the sides are nailed together. This method of nailing staggers the sides and forms a perfect square.

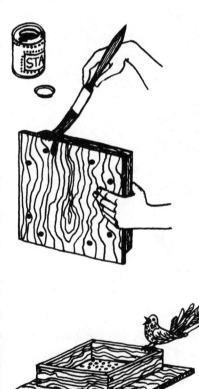

The next step in assembling the bird feeder is for you to measure and make a mark 2 inches from each of the four edges of the bottom square. Then place this bottom board on the frame so that the outline of the frame touches the 2-inch marks that you have just made. Nail the bottom board to the frame with the same size nails you used on the frame. In this case use two nails for each side of the frame.

The last step is to oil or stain the feeder. This coating protects it from the winter weather. Apply the linseed oil or stain with a brush and then wipe dry with a rag or paper towel.

Your bird feeder is now ready for you to nail to a post (a fence post will do) or wire to the branch of a tree. Put bread crumbs, seeds or suet in it every day during the winter, and you will be sure to attract birds.

3. HOT DISH COASTER

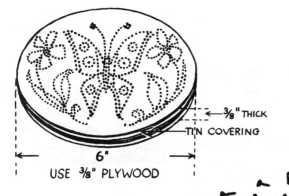

¾" THICK

TIN COVERING

6"

USE ⅜" PLYWOOD

Materials Needed

1 small jar of alcohol
1 small jar of orange shellac
1 small can of polishing wax
1 piece of paper 6" x 6"
1 piece of plywood ⅜" x 6" x 6"
1 large tin can at least 6" tall
60 ¼" bright steel wire nails
1 2" (6d) common nail

Tools Needed

1 small paintbrush, about ½"
1 ruler
1 pencil compass
1 pencil
1 coping saw
3 coping saw blades
1 claw hammer
1 pair of scissors
1 pair of tin snips
1 metal-working file with handle
1 woodworking file with handle

Your mother will appreciate a hot dish coaster that you make for her. You can make this of a strong thin wood called plywood. Plywood has been made in a shop from thin sheets of soft wood glued together at right angles. This prevents splitting and warping.

With a pencil compass, draw a 6-inch circle on your ⅜-inch-thick piece of plywood. To find the center of the plywood square, draw diagonal lines across it from corner to corner. The center of the circle is where the lines cross. Then place the point of your compass in the center and adjust the distance between the pencil point and metal point of the compass so that they are 3 inches apart. (This is the radius.) Then, when you spin the compass around, you will have a 6-inch circle, that is, a circle 6 inches in diameter.

Next, cut out the plywood circle with a coping saw. To keep the piece of plywood steady when you saw, put it in your vise or hold it down with one hand on your workbench or a strong box. Be sure to keep your saw on the outside of your line.

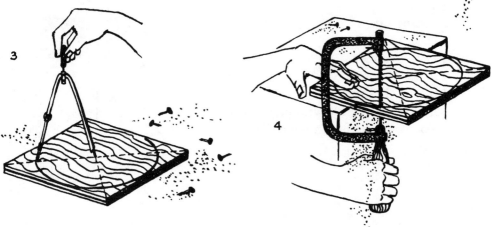

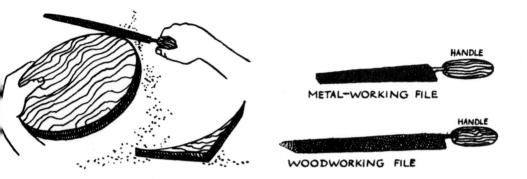

METAL-WORKING FILE

HANDLE

WOODWORKING FILE

HANDLE

When your circle has been cut out, smooth the edge with a woodworking file. As a safety measure, be sure you have a handle on your file. A file handle keeps the "tang" or sharp end of the file from stabbing your hand as you work. Continue to file the edge until it is nice and smooth.

You make the metal top of the coaster from a large tin can. First remove the top of the can completely, and with your tin snips cut down the seam of the can and then cut around the bottom. (A pair of ordinary scissors cannot be used for cutting tin as it is not strong enough.) Discard the bottom, and flatten the body of the can so you have a large flat piece of tin. Using the pencil compass again, draw a 5½-inch circle on the tin. (The metal tip of the compass should now measure half of 5½ inches, or 2¾ inches from the pencil point.) Cut this circle out with the tin snips.

File the tin circle smooth with a metal-working file. A metal-working file

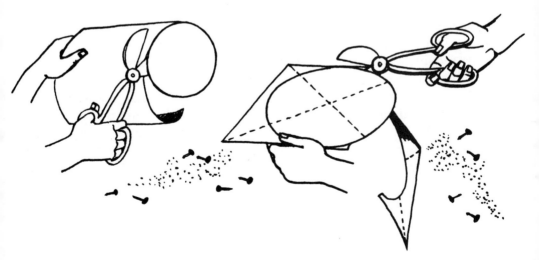

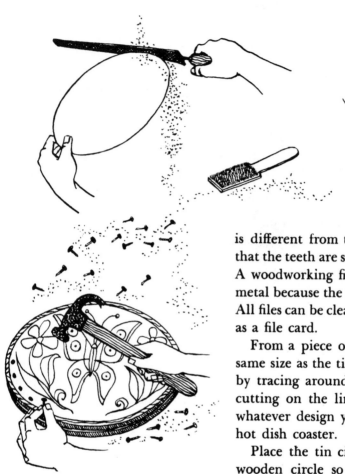

is different from the woodworking file in that the teeth are smaller and much harder. A woodworking file cannot be used to file metal because the metal will dull the teeth. All files can be cleaned with a brush known as a file card.

From a piece of paper, cut a circle the same size as the tin circle. You can do this by tracing around the tin circle and then cutting on the line. On this paper, draw whatever design you want to put on your hot dish coaster.

Place the tin circle, outside up, on the wooden circle so that there is a ¼-inch border all around. Then put the paper circle down. Using your small nails and a hammer, nail the edge of the paper and metal to the plywood. The nails should be ½-inch apart. Be sure to hold these circles down tight so that they don't slip out of place as you nail them on.

To make a tool for stamping your design in the metal, file off the point of a large nail until the end is smooth and round. With the picture you drew on the paper as your guide, tap the nail with a hammer along the lines of the design, spacing each dent an equal distance apart. Tap lightly so that you do not punch your tool all the way through the metal. After the design has been tapped in, tear off the paper. Put a coat of shellac on the wooden part of your coaster. After two hours, put on a second shellac coat. After you use your brush clean it in alcohol. After the second coat of shellac wait four hours for it to dry, and then polish the tin with a rag. You can give both the tin and wood a coat of wax and then polish both sides if you want them to shine brightly.

Hot dish coasters can be made in many shapes. Try making an oval one or a shape of your own design.

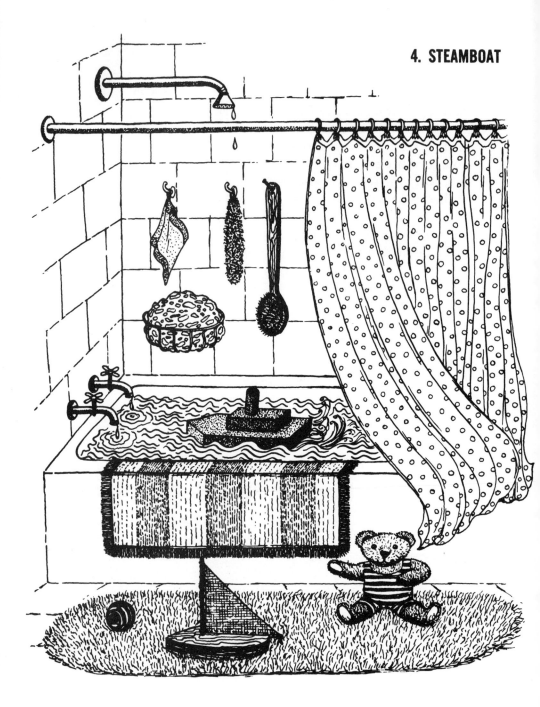

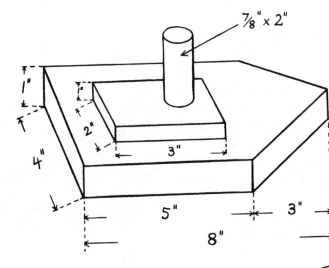

Materials Needed

- 1 piece of wood 1" x 4" x 8" or more
- 1 piece of wood 1" x 2" x 3"
- 1 dowel rod or broomstick ⅞" x 2"
- 2 1½" (4d) common nails
- 1 small can or tube of glue
- 2 small cans of enamel or paint
- 1 can of paint thinner or turpentine

Tools Needed

- 1 paintbrush about ½"
- 1 try square
- 1 crosscut saw
- 1 claw hammer
- 1 pencil
- 1 ⅞" auger bit
- 1 brace

In just an afternoon or evening, you can make a steamboat that floats. Very few tools are required. First collect the materials and tools listed above. Then you are ready to begin to build.

On a piece of wood 1 inch thick and 4 inches wide, measure a piece 8 inches long. With a pencil and try square, draw a line across the width of the board. Be sure to hold the head of the try square firmly against the edge of the board when drawing your line.

Cut the board on this line with a crosscut saw. This is the stern or back of the boat. To make the point or bow of the boat, measure 3 inches in from the other end and draw a line across with square and pencil. Then find the center of the 4-inch width by measuring in 2 inches from the side edge. Draw a line the length of the board. Mark the point where it touches the bow. From it draw straight lines to the ends of the line you drew at the 3-inch mark. This will give you a

triangle for a bow. Cut off on both of these lines with your saw. Now your bow is complete.

Cut the cabin from a 1-inch by 2-inch board. Measure off a piece 3 inches long. For the measuring, use your try square and pencil and cut off with the same saw that you used before.

Draw a line down the length of the cabin roof in the center —1 inch from each side. On this

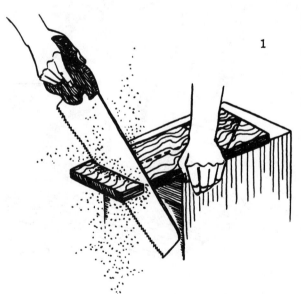

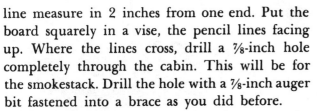

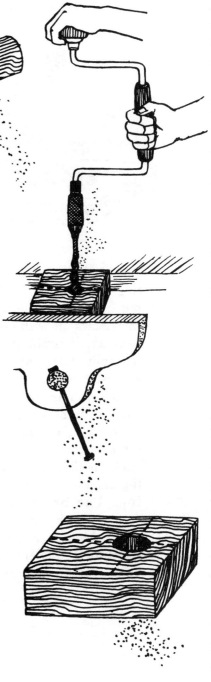

line measure in 2 inches from one end. Put the board squarely in a vise, the pencil lines facing up. Where the lines cross, drill a ⅞-inch hole completely through the cabin. This will be for the smokestack. Drill the hole with a ⅞-inch auger bit fastened into a brace as you did before.

Now take the larger board and measure in, marking with your pencil, 1 inch from the stern and also 1 inch from each side to locate the place for the cabin. Coat the cabin bottom with glue and place the cabin on the marks so that the hole for the smokestack faces the bow. Nail on with 1½ inch (4d) nails.

Make the smokestack from a ⅞-inch dowel rod (see page 31) or broomstick.

For this smokestack you need to cut off a piece 2 inches long.

Check to see if the smokestack will fit into the hole. If it will not, whittle the bottom edges of the rod with a pocketknife until it does. Be sure to whittle away from your body. Put some glue on one end of the smokestack and tap it into place with your claw hammer or a mallet. A mallet is a

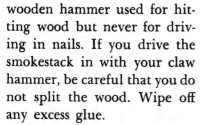

wooden hammer used for hitting wood but never for driving in nails. If you drive the smokestack in with your claw hammer, be careful that you do not split the wood. Wipe off any excess glue.

Now you are ready to paint your steamboat. You might want to paint the hull and cabin one color and the smokestack another. Be sure to stir the paint or enamel before using. The brush has to be cleaned with turpentine or paint thinner each time you use it for a different color and before you put it away.

5. TOY SLED

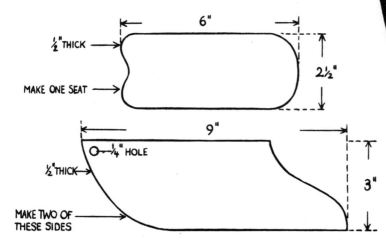

6"

½" THICK

2½"

MAKE ONE SEAT

9"

O—¼" HOLE

½" THICK

3"

MAKE TWO OF
THESE SIDES

Materials Needed
1 sheet of medium sandpaper
1 piece of wood ½" x 3" x 18"
1 piece of wood ½" x 2½" x 6"
1 piece of paper 3" x 9"
1 piece of paper 2½" x 6"
4 1⅛" (2d) common nails
1 piece of heavy twine or thin rope 6' long
2 small cans of paint or enamel
1 small can of paint thinner or turpentine

1 coping saw
3 coping saw blades
1 claw hammer
1 ½″ paintbrush
1 1/16″ paintbrush
1 pencil
1 hand drill
1 ⅛″ twist drill
1 pair of scissors
1 ruler

Before you begin to build, gather the materials and tools needed for your project.

Start out by making two patterns — one for the runners and one for the seat. On the 3-inch by 9-inch piece of paper, sketch a wooden sled runner as shown in the illustration. On the 2½-inch by 6-inch piece of paper, sketch the seat. Cut out both patterns.

Place the runner pattern close to one end of your ½-inch by 3-inch by 18-inch board and trace around the outline. Then move the pattern to the other end of the board and trace again. Place the seat pattern on the ½-inch by 2½-inch by 6-inch board and trace.

Cut out all three pieces with a coping saw, using a vise and workbench or a steady box to lean on.

Sandpaper your pieces smooth with medium sandpaper. Be sure to rub the sandpaper with the grain, not against it. To make runners slide better on the snow, round them off with sandpaper. You can do this by wrapping the sandpaper around a block of wood.

One-half inch from the top and 2 inches from the front edge of each runner, draw a line. The line should end 2 inches from the back edge. This shows where the top of the seat should be when the sled is put together. Then nail the runners to the seat (see left below), using two 1⅛-inch (2d) common nails for each runner. Drive these nails in with your claw hammer.

For rope holes, use a ⅛-inch twist drill in a hand drill to make a small hole in the front point of each runner (see page 39). The hand drill holds the twist drill which does the actual drilling. To put a twist drill in a hand drill, unscrew the jaws, insert the drill and tighten. To drill, hold the drill handle in your left hand, push the twist drill against the wood, and crank with your right hand.

Thread one end of the twine or rope through each of the holes and then tie each end separately.

You will want to give this sled one or two coats of

your favorite color, paint or enamel. This will protect the wood and make your toy look better. Enamel is usually a little glossier and tougher than paint. Use turpentine to thin the paint and help it dry. Linseed oil helps paint to flow on smoothly and dry to a glossy finish. Let the first coat dry overnight before applying the second. While the sled dries, you can hang the sled up by its rope. If you want to decorate the sled with another color you can paint a name on the seat or decorations on the side of the run-

ners as shown in the illustration. The best way to do this is to sketch the name and design on the sled with soft white chalk. Then use the small (1/16-inch) brush to paint the letters on.

If you want to make a gift for a friend or sister or brother, why not make this little sled? It will be fun in the winter when it snows.

6. TIE RACK

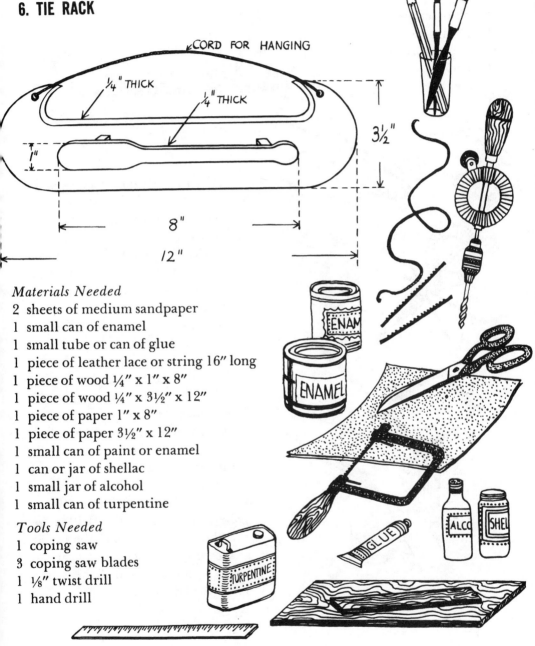

CORD FOR HANGING

¼" THICK

¼" THICK

3½"

1"

8"

12"

Materials Needed

2 sheets of medium sandpaper
1 small can of enamel
1 small tube or can of glue
1 piece of leather lace or string 16" long
1 piece of wood ¼" x 1" x 8"
1 piece of wood ¼" x 3½" x 12"
1 piece of paper 1" x 8"
1 piece of paper 3½" x 12"
1 small can of paint or enamel
1 can or jar of shellac
1 small jar of alcohol
1 small can of turpentine

Tools Needed

1 coping saw
3 coping saw blades
1 ⅛" twist drill
1 hand drill

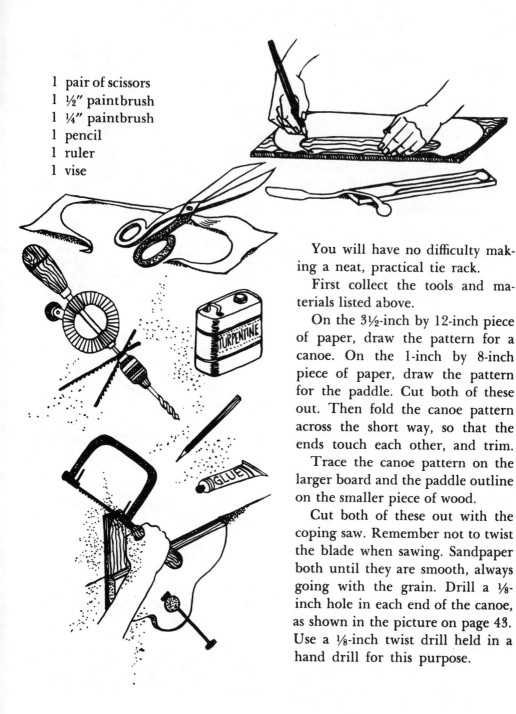

1 pair of scissors
1 ½″ paintbrush
1 ¼″ paintbrush
1 pencil
1 ruler
1 vise

You will have no difficulty making a neat, practical tie rack.

First collect the tools and materials listed above.

On the 3½-inch by 12-inch piece of paper, draw the pattern for a canoe. On the 1-inch by 8-inch piece of paper, draw the pattern for the paddle. Cut both of these out. Then fold the canoe pattern across the short way, so that the ends touch each other, and trim.

Trace the canoe pattern on the larger board and the paddle outline on the smaller piece of wood.

Cut both of these out with the coping saw. Remember not to twist the blade when sawing. Sandpaper both until they are smooth, always going with the grain. Drill a ⅛-inch hole in each end of the canoe, as shown in the picture on page 43. Use a ⅛-inch twist drill held in a hand drill for this purpose.

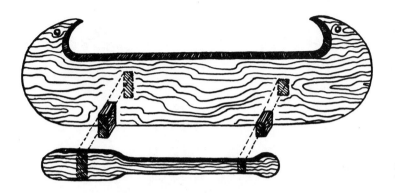

Using the remaining portion of the board from which you patterned the canoe, cut two wooden blocks (see above). These will hold the paddle in place on the canoe. Then smooth these blocks by rubbing them on a sheet of sandpaper. Put glue on both of the small ends of these blocks. Space the blocks on the canoe and place the paddle on the blocks as shown in the picture. Allow them to dry overnight. Be sure to use wood glue. Many wood glues are made from fish, bones or milk. In this and certain other cases, wood glue will hold the pieces together and you do not need nails or screws.

To make the tie rack more attractive, shellac the paddle and give the canoe a coat of paint or enamel. If one coat is not enough, paint the canoe twice, but be sure to allow a day between coats. Brushes should be cleaned very carefully after each use.

Now you are ready for the finishing touch. Fasten the string to each end of the canoe by tying it through the holes you drilled there.

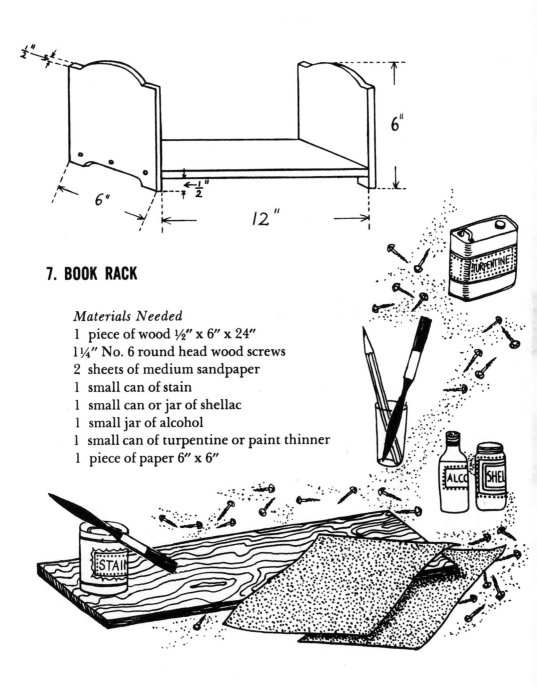

7. BOOK RACK

Materials Needed

1 piece of wood ½″ x 6″ x 24″
1¼″ No. 6 round head wood screws
2 sheets of medium sandpaper
1 small can of stain
1 small can or jar of shellac
1 small jar of alcohol
1 small can of turpentine or paint thinner
1 piece of paper 6″ x 6″

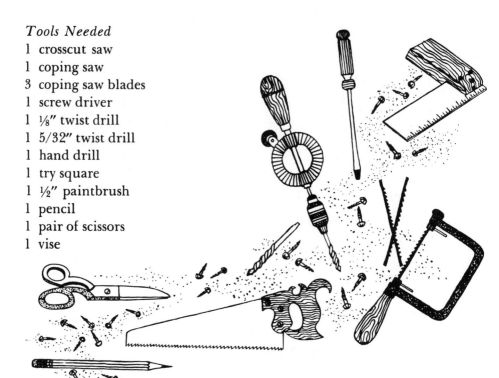

Tools Needed

1 crosscut saw
1 coping saw
3 coping saw blades
1 screw driver
1 ⅛" twist drill
1 5/32" twist drill
1 hand drill
1 try square
1 ½" paintbrush
1 pencil
1 pair of scissors
1 vise

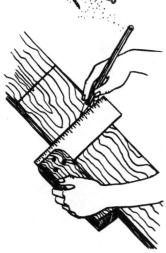

This handy book rack is ideal for use on a desk or table. You can make it of pine or any other soft wood.

Measure off two 6-inch pieces of wood using your try square (see p. 85). Then place the try square on the board so that the head rests on the edge and the blade crosses one of the lines that you just measured. Mark with your pencil. Mark off the second piece in the same way.

Cut on the lines with your crosscut saw. To start your saw cut, place the saw on the mark and pull up before you push down. This will start your cut at the right spot. Try to keep your saw straight. You can do this if you hold the saw firmly and guide it with one hand while your other hand holds the board. The ½-inch by 6-inch by 12-inch piece of wood that is left is the piece used for the base of the book rack.

Draw the pattern for the ends of the book rack on your 6-inch by 6-inch piece of paper. Cut out, fold down the center, and trim so that both sides will be exactly even. Trace the pattern on both wooden ends.

Cut out the ends with your coping saw. Work slowly and keep the saw moving back and forth as you turn the blade. Try to follow the line carefully. This will avoid rough edges. Sandpaper all the places where you made cuts until they are smooth.

Measure up ½-inch from the bottom of the inside of each end and mark this spot. Draw a line completely across, using the try

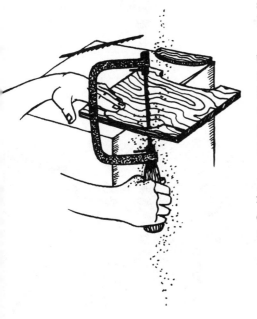

square. This is where your bottom board will rest.

Measure up ¾-inch from the bottom of the front of both ends and mark in the same way. Then measure in 1 inch, 3 inches and 5 inches from one end of this line. These will be the points where your screws will be placed.

At each of these six marks that you just made, drill a 5/32-inch hole (see next page), using the 5/32-inch twist drill and hand drill (see p. 12). Drill the hole all the way through. Place these ends on the base (one at a time) on the lines you drew before. Then mark where these holes touch the base. Drill each hole about 2 inches deep in the base, using the 1/8-inch twist drill and hand drill. These holes in the base will guide in the screws.

Now fasten the ends on the base with your round head screws. The screws fit through the holes in the ends and are then screwed into the base until they are in tightly. You do this by holding the screw with your left hand. With your right hand, put the bit of the screw driver blade in the screw slot and turn the entire screw driver clockwise. As you already know, screw drivers are used for putting in screws. You also need to know that they come in different sizes. The bit of the screw driver blade should just fit into the slot of the screw.

Sandpaper any marks or rough spots and give the book rack a coat of stain. Wipe the stain off and apply two coats of shellac.

8. TABLE LAMP

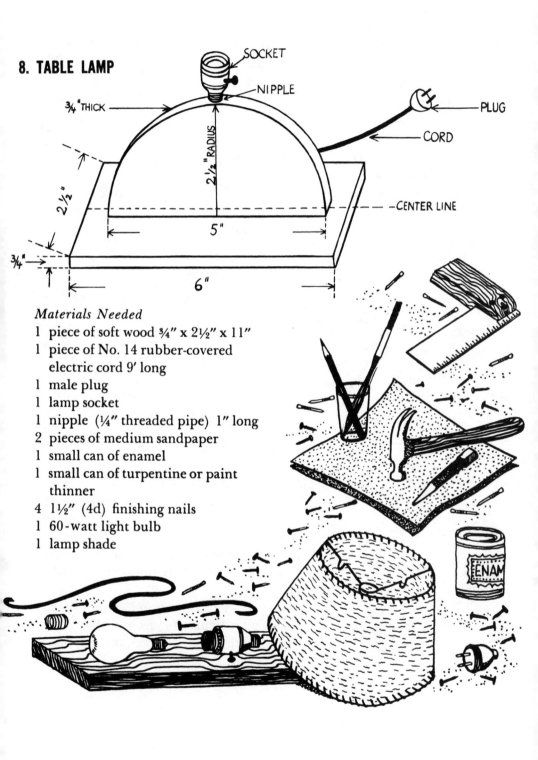

SOCKET

NIPPLE

PLUG

CORD

¾" THICK

2½" RADIUS

CENTER LINE

2½"

¾"

5"

6"

Materials Needed

1 piece of soft wood ¾" x 2½" x 11"
1 piece of No. 14 rubber-covered electric cord 9' long
1 male plug
1 lamp socket
1 nipple (¼" threaded pipe) 1" long
2 pieces of medium sandpaper
1 small can of enamel
1 small can of turpentine or paint thinner
4 1½" (4d) finishing nails
1 60-watt light bulb
1 lamp shade

1 claw hammer
1 crosscut saw
1 coping saw
3 coping saw blades
1 ¼″ paintbrush
1 pencil compass
1 5/16″ auger bit
1 brace
1 pencil
1 try square
1 nail set

An electric table lamp is easier to make than you may think. It is important to assemble all your tools and materials before you begin to build.

You can make an electric lamp from a piece of soft wood ¾ inch by 2½ inches by 11 inches. First, measure 6 inches from a good end and draw a line straight across, using your try square (see p. 85) and pencil. Cut on the edge of this line with the crosscut saw. This completes the bottom of the lamp.

Locate the center of your 5-inch long board by marking a point 2½″ from a short end. Set your compass at 2½ inches, put the metal

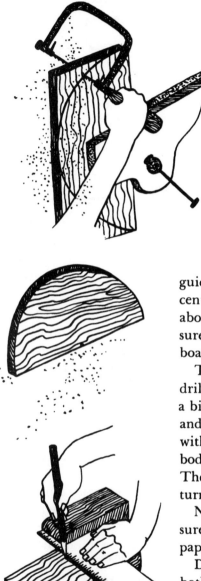

point on the wood at this point and draw a half circle. Cut on the outside of this line with a coping saw.

Measure 2½ inches in from one end of the straight side of the half circle. From that point draw a line across the width to the top of the arc. At the place where this line meets the top edge, measure in ⅜ of an inch. This gives you the center of the top. Put the 5/16-inch auger bit in the brace and drill a hole through the half circle from the top to the bottom (see page 52). Be sure to keep the auger bit in line with your guide line. Then drill another hole in from the center of one side to meet this hole, at a place about one inch from the bottom of the circle. Be sure that you do not go all the way through the board but stop at the hole.

The bits that fit into the brace actually do the drilling. They are known as auger bits. To put a bit into a brace, open the jaws, slide in the bit, and tighten. To use hold the brace near the bit with your left hand, place the knob against your body, and grasp the handle with your right hand. Then push the screw of the bit into the wood and turn the handle clockwise.

Now is the time to sandpaper both pieces. Be sure you smooth off all rough spots and only sandpaper with the grain of the wood.

Draw a line the long way down the center of both sides of the base. This means the line will be 1¼ inches in from the edge. Draw a line down the center of the underside of the half circle, also

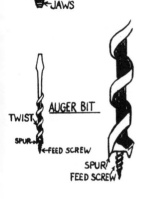

the long way, and extend this line up the side a little bit. Measure in ½ inch from both ends of the base and make a mark. Now place the bottom on the circle by matching up the lines. Nail in place with four 1½ inch (4d) finishing nails. Then drive the nail heads below the surface of the wood by using a nail set. Place the point of the nail set on the head of the nail and then hit it with a hammer until the nail head is below the surface.

If you have had no experience wiring electric lamps or handling sockets and plugs, ask an adult to help you with the next few steps.

Screw the nipple (threaded pipe) in the top of the circle, and the lamp socket on the thread. Separate the top portion (receptacle) of the lamp socket from the base. Thread the electric cord through the wooden portion of the lamp. Scrape the insulation off both

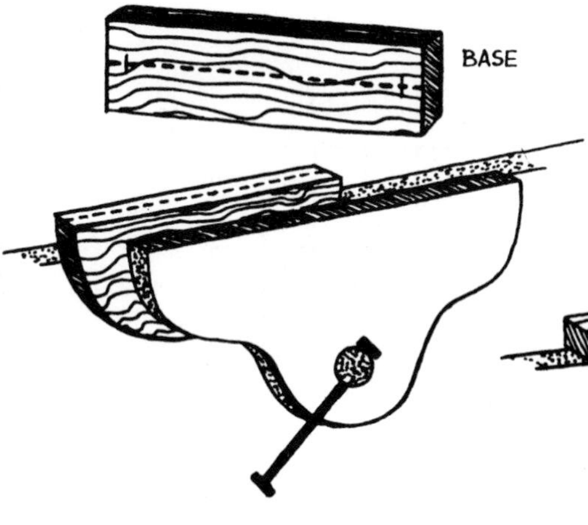

BASE

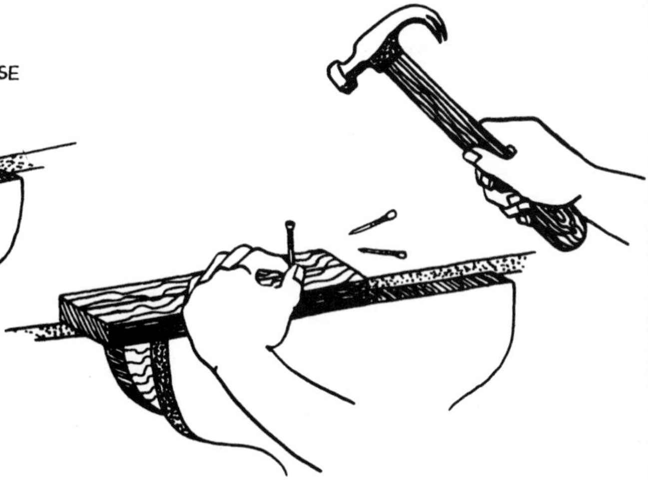

wires at each end of the cord. Connect the wires to the socket and male plug. After your lamp has been inspected, you can test it by plugging it into the electricity.

Give the entire lamp a coat of stain and then wipe dry with a rag. Apply two coats of shellac.

Put a small shade on your table lamp and it is ready to use.

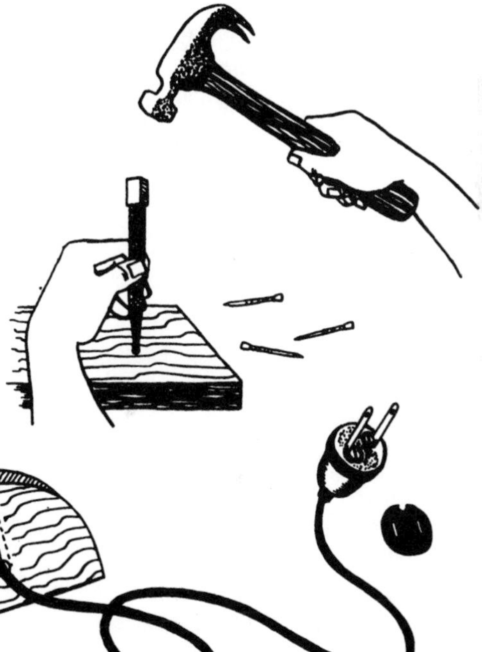

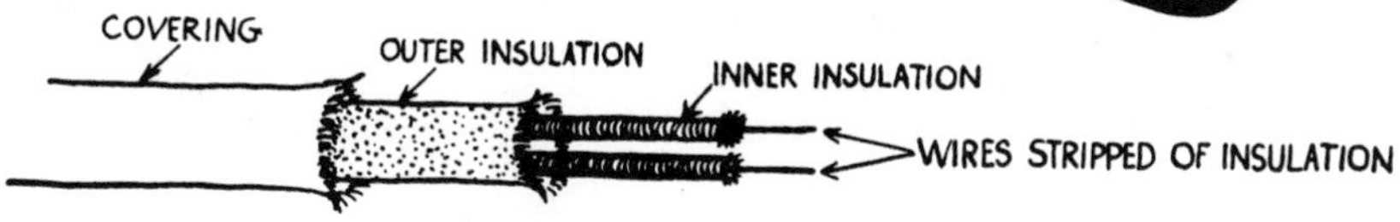

COVERING   OUTER INSULATION   INNER INSULATION

WIRES STRIPPED OF INSULATION

ELECTRIC CORD

9. CLOCK SHELF

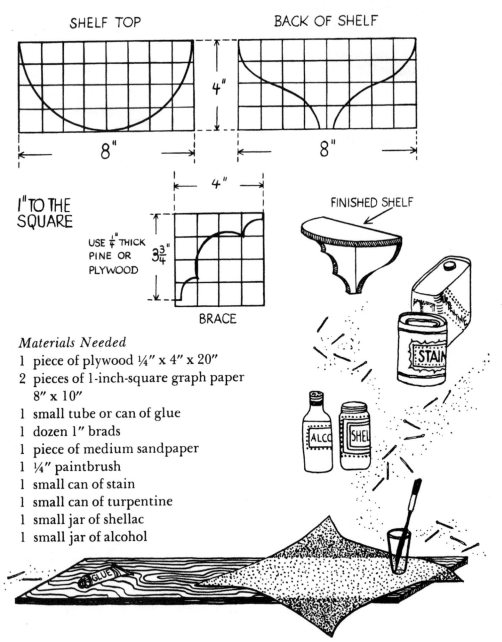

SHELF TOP

BACK OF SHELF

4"

8"

8"

1" TO THE
SQUARE

USE ¼" THICK
PINE OR
PLYWOOD

4"

3¾"

BRACE

FINISHED SHELF

STAIN

ALCO   SHEL

GLUE

Materials Needed

1 piece of plywood ¼" x 4" x 20"
2 pieces of 1-inch-square graph paper
   8" x 10"
1 small tube or can of glue
1 dozen 1" brads
1 piece of medium sandpaper
1 ¼" paintbrush
1 small can of stain
1 small can of turpentine
1 small jar of shellac
1 small jar of alcohol

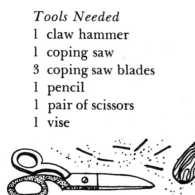

1 claw hammer
1 coping saw
3 coping saw blades
1 pencil
1 pair of scissors
1 vise

In making this clock shelf you have an opportunity to be your own designer. After gathering all the tools and materials you will need, cut two pieces of the 1-inch-squared graph paper 4 inches by 8 inches, and one piece 4 inches by 4 inches. Measure it by counting the squares. On one of the larger pieces of graph paper draw the shape you want for the top of your shelf, and on the other draw the shape for the back of the shelf. On the smaller piece of paper draw the shape of the brace. Use the squares as guide lines and be sure the left side is always the same size and design as

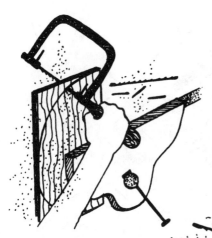

the right. Cut out all three patterns with your scissors.

Trace all three patterns on the ¼-inch by 4-inch by 20-inch piece of plywood. Line up a straight edge of each pattern with a straight edge of the plywood board.

Clamp the plywood board into the vise. Use your coping saw to cut out all of the pieces. Make your cuts slowly and evenly, being careful not to split the plywood. After you have cut out all three pieces, sandpaper all the edges until they are smooth.

Draw a light line across the inside center of the top and back piece's short sides. Use your graph paper as a guide. These lines provide guides when assembling the shelf.

Put a coat of glue on the top edge of the shelf back. Set the shelf top on it and then nail in place with about

five brads. Brads are small finishing nails, which will not split the wood. Tap the heads even with the surface of the wood. Put a coat of glue on the inside edges of the brace, set the brace between the top and back pieces and nail the top and back to the brace with about three nails each. Wipe off any excess glue.

Give your shelf a coat of stain and then wipe dry. Follow with two coats of shellac. Allow at least two hours between each coat.

You now have completed your clock shelf. Check with Mom or Dad as to where you can put it up in your house.

10. CANDLESTICKS

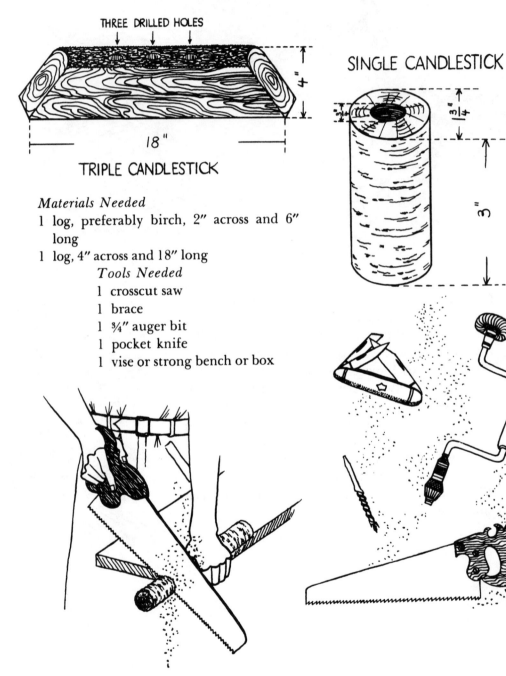

THREE DRILLED HOLES

4"

18"

TRIPLE CANDLESTICK

SINGLE CANDLESTICK

1¾"

3"

Materials Needed

1 log, preferably birch, 2″ across and 6″ long

1 log, 4″ across and 18″ long

Tools Needed

1 crosscut saw

1 brace

1 ¾″ auger bit

1 pocket knife

1 vise or strong bench or box

You can make many woodworking projects from logs and sticks. These candlesticks are just two of the possibilities.

The pair of candlesticks is made by cutting two 3-inch sections from a log that measures about 2 inches across. This is done with a crosscut saw. Then drill a ¾-inch hole about 1 inch deep in the center of one end of each log. You drill the hole with a ¾-inch auger bit held in a brace.

The triple candlestick is made by cutting an 18-inch section from a 4-inch wide log. Then whittle the bottom flat with a pocket knife. When whittling, be sure to whittle away from your body. Cut off each of the ends at a slant as shown in the picture. This is done best with a crosscut saw. Drill three ¾-inch

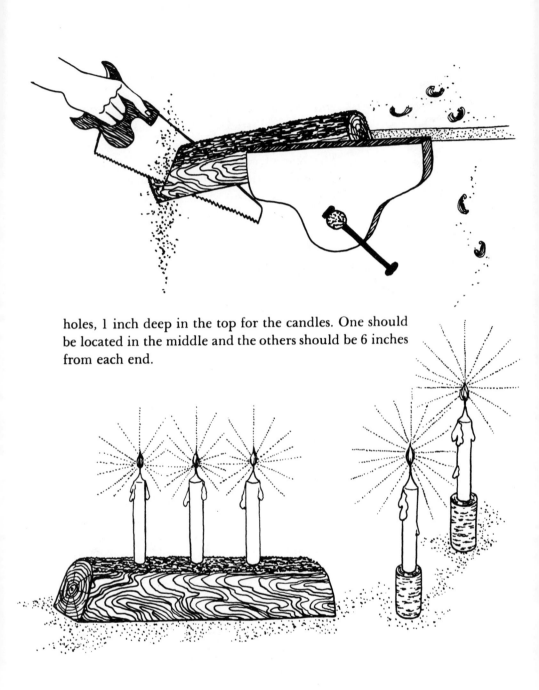

holes, 1 inch deep in the top for the candles. One should be located in the middle and the others should be 6 inches from each end.

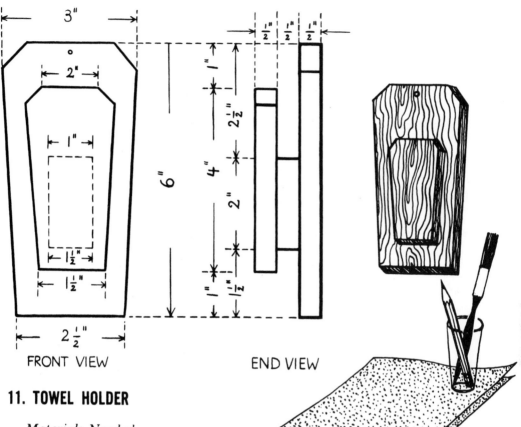

FRONT VIEW   END VIEW

11. TOWEL HOLDER

Materials Needed

1 piece of soft wood ½″ x 3″ x 6″
1 piece of soft wood ½″ x 2″ x 5″
1 small tube or can of wood glue
1 can of enamel
1 small can of turpentine or paint thinner
1 piece of paper 3″ x 6″
1 piece of paper 2″ x 4″
2 pieces of medium sandpaper

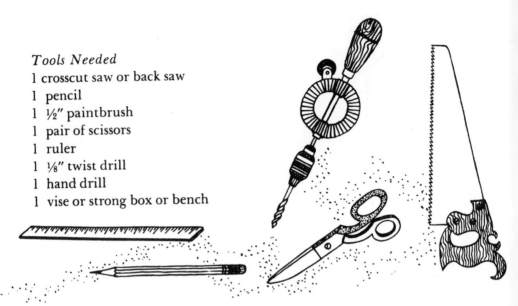

Tools Needed

1 crosscut saw or back saw
1 pencil
1 ½" paintbrush
1 pair of scissors
1 ruler
1 ⅛" twist drill
1 hand drill
1 vise or strong box or bench

You can make this towel rack from your own pattern. First, prepare the necessary equipment. Then draw a pattern for the front on a 2-inch by 4-inch piece of paper and a pattern for the back on a 3-inch by 6-inch piece of paper. Cut both of these patterns out with your scissors, fold down the center the long way, and trim to make certain they are even.

For this project you should use a soft wood such as Douglas fir, pine, cypress or spruce. These are best when doing hand woodworking.

Use your ruler to measure off

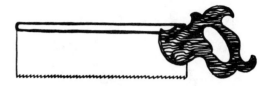

BACK SAW

FROM THE SIDE

FROM BELOW

a 1-inch piece of the ½-inch by 2-inch by 5-inch board. Then cut this piece off with a crosscut or back saw. A back saw, a saw with a very stiff back, is used in cabinet-making for cuts both with and against the grain. The teeth of the saw are a combination of crosscut and rip teeth.

Trace the patterns for the front piece on the smaller board, and the pattern for the back piece on the larger board. Cut out with either a crosscut or back saw. Sandpaper all pieces carefully.

Coat both sides of the small 1-inch by 2-inch block with glue and place it 1½″ from the bottom and in the center of the back piece. Then place the front piece on this small block so that it

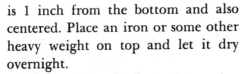

is 1 inch from the bottom and also centered. Place an iron or some other heavy weight on top and let it dry overnight.

The next day, scrape off any glue that shows. Drill a hole with the ⅛-inch twist drill and hand drill (see p. 12) in the center of the back, ½ inch down from the top.

Give the rack two coats of enamel, allowing the first coat to dry overnight before applying the second.

Your towel rack is now ready to be put on the wall.

12. CART

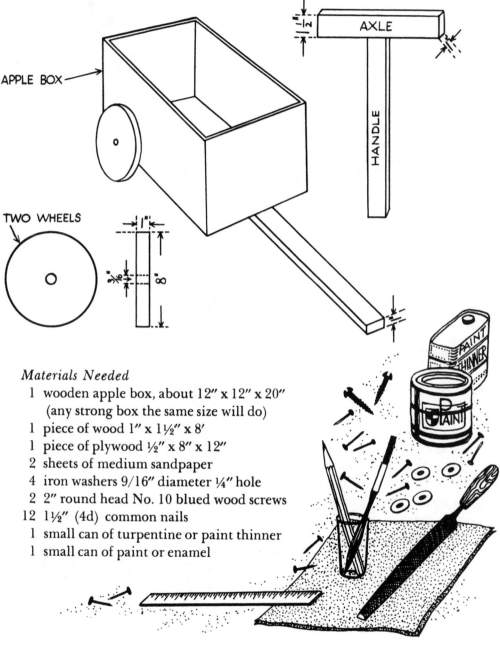

APPLE BOX

AXLE

HANDLE

TWO WHEELS

Materials Needed

1 wooden apple box, about 12" x 12" x 20"
  (any strong box the same size will do)
1 piece of wood 1" x 1½" x 8'
1 piece of plywood ½" x 8" x 12"
2 sheets of medium sandpaper
4 iron washers 9/16" diameter ¼" hole
2 2" round head No. 10 blued wood screws
12 1½" (4d) common nails
1 small can of turpentine or paint thinner
1 small can of paint or enamel

1 claw hammer
1 try square
1 hand drill
1 3/16″ twist drill
1 5/32″ twist drill
1 ½″ paintbrush
1 pencil compass
1 pencil
1 yardstick or ruler
1 half-round woodworking file with
  handle
1 crosscut saw
1 coping saw
3 coping saw blades
1 screw driver

There are many interesting projects that can be made from materials found around the house or obtained from the local stores. This cart is such a project, for it is made from an apple box. Get a strong box, one that does not have split boards. Lay out the other materials listed above.

For the axle, cut from the 1-inch by 1½-inch by 8-feet strip of wood, a piece that is 2 inches longer than the box is wide. The handle piece should be made from the same strip and needs to be about 5 or 6 feet long.

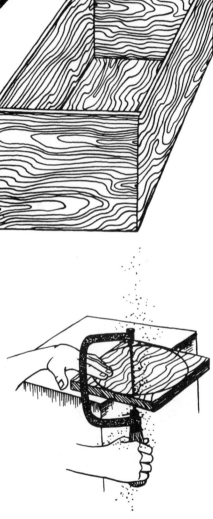

Measure these lengths with a yardstick. If you have one, a yardstick which is 36 inches or 3 feet long is easier to use on this project. However, a ruler can be used very satisfactorily. In each case, draw your line across with a try square and pencil. Make these cuts with your crosscut saw.

To make the wheels, you first draw two 8-inch circles on the plywood. This is done by setting the point of the compass 4 inches from the point of the pencil. When the compass is spun around on the wood with the metal point in the center you have an 8-inch circle.

Cut out both wheels with your coping saw. Then file smooth with a woodworking file. Be sure that you have a

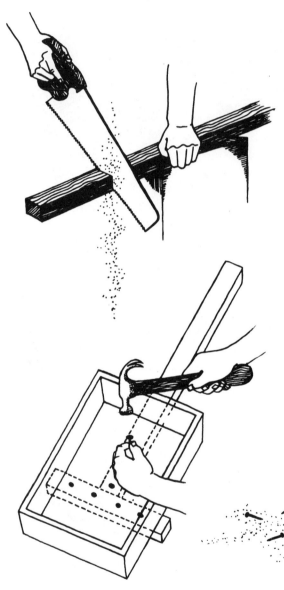

handle on the file. File around the wheels, not across. If you go across you may split off the outer layer of plywood. Next, sandpaper all the parts, including the box.

Place the bottom of the box on the axle so that the axle is about ⅓ the way from one end of the box and extends over each side about 1 inch. Then nail the bottom of the box to the axle.

Next place the bottom of the box on the handle so that the handle goes down the middle of the box bottom and hits the axle. Nail in place. It will take about four nails.

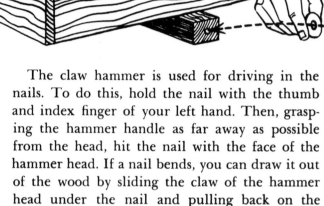

The claw hammer is used for driving in the nails. To do this, hold the nail with the thumb and index finger of your left hand. Then, grasping the hammer handle as far away as possible from the head, hit the nail with the face of the hammer head. If a nail bends, you can draw it out of the wood by sliding the claw of the hammer head under the nail and pulling back on the handle.

Drill a 3/16-inch hole through the center of each wheel at the spot marked by the compass point. This is done with your 3/16-inch twist drill mounted in the hand drill. Drill a 5/32-inch hole in the center of each end of the wooden axle. Do this by using the 5/32-inch twist drill in the hand drill. This will make a pilot hole for the screws.

Place a washer, a wheel, and then another washer on each round head screw. Then screw these through the pilot holes and into the ends of the axles with the screw driver. These 2-inch

round head (No. 10 blued) wood screws are made of steel and are very strong.

Give the entire wagon a coat of paint. When painting, do the wheels, outside bottom, inside of box, outside of box and handle in that order. Clean your brush after using, in turpentine or paint thinner. Be sure all paint rags are placed in metal containers as soon as you have finished using them.

13. BIRDHOUSE FOR A WREN

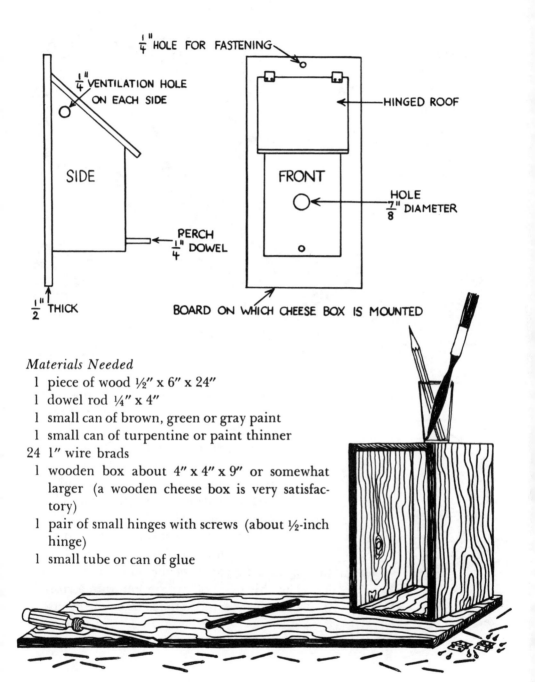

$\frac{1}{4}''$ HOLE FOR FASTENING

$\frac{1}{4}''$ VENTILATION HOLE ON EACH SIDE

SIDE

FRONT

HINGED ROOF

HOLE $\frac{7}{8}''$ DIAMETER

PERCH $\frac{1}{4}''$ DOWEL

$\frac{1}{2}''$ THICK

BOARD ON WHICH CHEESE BOX IS MOUNTED

Materials Needed

1 piece of wood ½″ x 6″ x 24″
1 dowel rod ¼″ x 4″
1 small can of brown, green or gray paint
1 small can of turpentine or paint thinner
24 1″ wire brads
1 wooden box about 4″ x 4″ x 9″ or somewhat larger (a wooden cheese box is very satisfactory)
1 pair of small hinges with screws (about ½-inch hinge)
1 small tube or can of glue

71

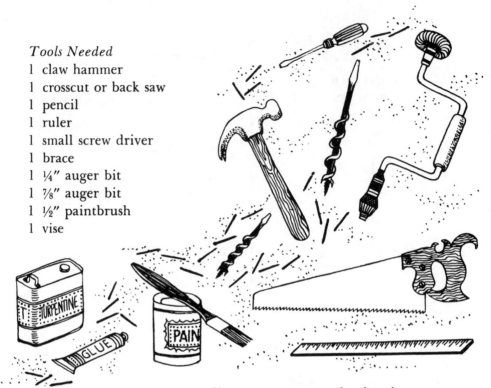

Tools Needed

1 claw hammer
1 crosscut or back saw
1 pencil
1 ruler
1 small screw driver
1 brace
1 ¼" auger bit
1 ⅞" auger bit
1 ½" paintbrush
1 vise

You can turn a wooden box into a very fine birdhouse. If you cannot find a cheese box of about 4 inches by 4 inches by 9 inches, a slightly larger box will do.

First, prepare the tools and materials.

To make the house, cut off one end of the box on a slant to form the roof. This is done by measuring down one side as many inches as the box is wide. Then draw a line from this point on the open side of box to the corner of the other closed side. Cut this piece off on the line with a crosscut or back saw. Do the same on the reverse side.

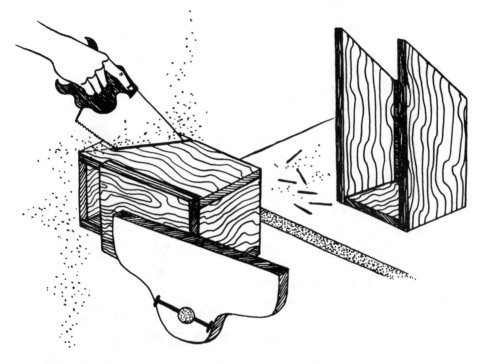

Make the back 2 inches wider and 2 inches longer than the box. The roof is made 1 inch wider and 1 inch longer than the part of the box that is to be covered. Drill a $\frac{7}{8}$-inch hole right in the center of the side of the box that will be the front of your birdhouse. A $\frac{1}{4}$-inch hole is drilled at the bottom of this same side for the perch. In the peak of each side drill a $\frac{1}{4}$-inch hole for ventilation. Another $\frac{1}{4}$-inch hole is drilled in the center of

the mounting board, ¾ of an inch down from the top. This provides a means of fastening the birdhouse to a tree or post. When drilling, drill slowly and easily so that you *drill* through and do not *push* the auger bit through the wood. If you push too hard when you are just about through, the wood will split.

Using the 1-inch brads, nail the backboard to your box. Fasten the roof to the backboard by means of the small hinges. This hinged roof makes it possible to clean out the

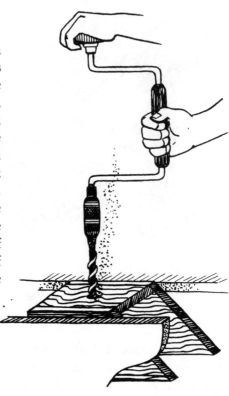

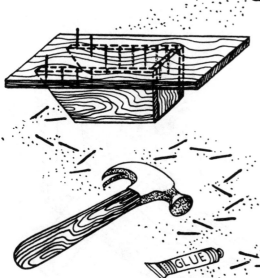

house at the end of each season. Look at the illustration to see how this is done. Glue the perch in the hole at the bottom of the box.

As a finishing touch, give the entire house and mounting board a coat of green, brown or gray paint.

In early spring put up your birdhouse so that it faces south. This can be done by fastening it to a tree or post with a large nail, screw or piece of wire going through the hole that you drilled in the top of the mounting board. To keep birds around, provide bread crumbs, suet and seeds, as well as plenty of water.

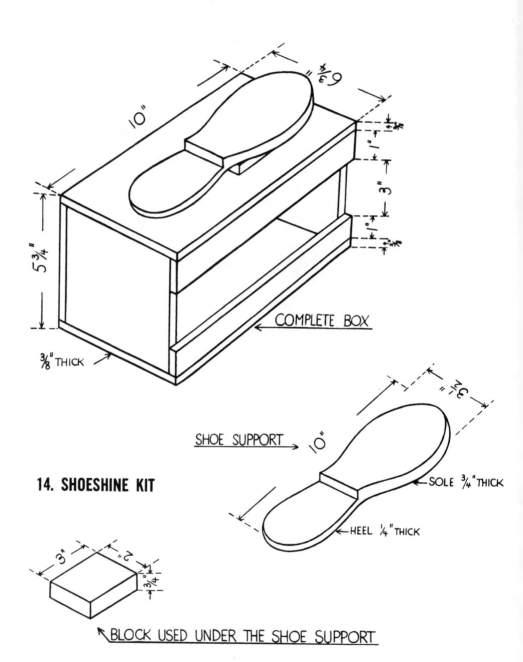

COMPLETE BOX

10"

6 3/4"

5 3/4"

3/8" THICK

1"

3"

1"

3/8"

3/8"

SHOE SUPPORT

10"

3 1/2"

1"

SOLE 3/4" THICK

HEEL 1/4" THICK

14. SHOESHINE KIT

3"

2"

3/4"

BLOCK USED UNDER THE SHOE SUPPORT

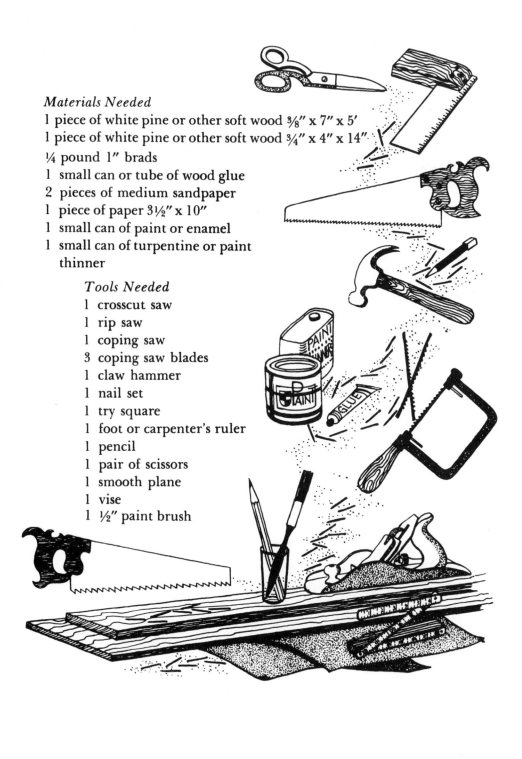

Materials Needed

1 piece of white pine or other soft wood ⅜" x 7" x 5'
1 piece of white pine or other soft wood ¾" x 4" x 14"
¼ pound 1" brads
1 small can or tube of wood glue
2 pieces of medium sandpaper
1 piece of paper 3½" x 10"
1 small can of paint or enamel
1 small can of turpentine or paint thinner

Tools Needed

1 crosscut saw
1 rip saw
1 coping saw
3 coping saw blades
1 claw hammer
1 nail set
1 try square
1 foot or carpenter's ruler
1 pencil
1 pair of scissors
1 smooth plane
1 vise
1 ½" paint brush

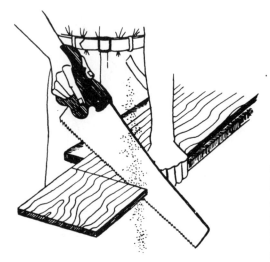

The complete shoeshine kit is made up of a box and wooden shoe. For the box you need:

2 ends ⅜" x 5" x 6"
1 top ⅜" x 6¾" x 10"
1 bottom ⅜" x 6¾" x 10"
1 side ⅜" x 5" x 10"
2 side strips ⅜" x 1" x 10"

All of these pieces are cut from a piece of white pine or other soft wood ⅜-inch by 7 inches by 5 feet. Make each of these pieces one at a time by first cutting a piece off your large board, 1 inch longer than needed. Do your measuring with a 1-foot ruler or a carpenter's ruler. A carpenter's ruler is a 1-foot ruler that folds up into a 6-inch package. Then follow the directions for squaring a block of wood on page 85. Follow the directions carefully for each piece.

Draw a shoe pattern on your piece of paper by tracing around your own shoe. Fold the shoe pattern down the middle, lengthwise, and trim. Trace the pattern on your ¾-inch by 4-inch piece of wood and cut out with the coping saw. Draw one line across where the heel meets the sole and another around the heel in the middle. (See next page, top drawing.) Then cut out the top heel section with

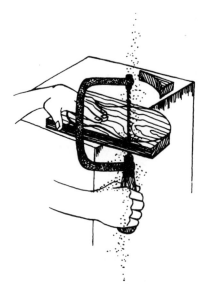

your coping saw. Sandpaper the entire shoe. From the piece of wood that is left, cut a piece 2 inches by 3 inches. Again follow the steps in squaring a block of wood on page 85.

Study the drawing of the complete shoeshine kit to see where all the pieces go. Glue and nail the block to the center of the underpart of the shoe. Put glue on the block and then

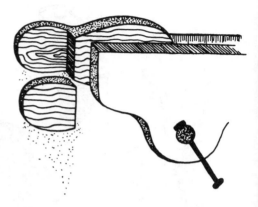

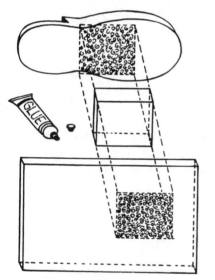

nail the top piece of the box to the block. Have the shoe and block centered lengthwise with the toe of the shoe extending over the front end of the box about 1 inch. Then nail all other pieces to the ends in this order: bottom, top, large side piece, and small side pieces. Set the heads of all nails below the surface with a nail set (see p. 12). Use putty or plastic wood to fill up any holes or cracks. Sandpaper the entire box; be sure that you go with the grain of the wood.

Give the kit two coats of oil paint or enamel. Allow 24 hours between coats. For complete directions on how to do this, see the section on wood finishing on page 89.

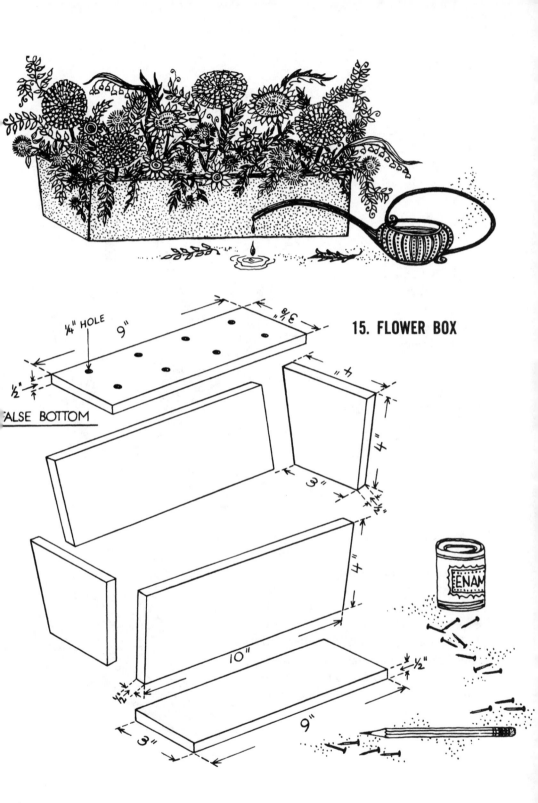

15. FLOWER BOX

¼" HOLE

9"

3/8"

½"

FALSE BOTTOM

4"

4"

3"

½"

4"

10"

½"

9"

3"

½"

ENAM

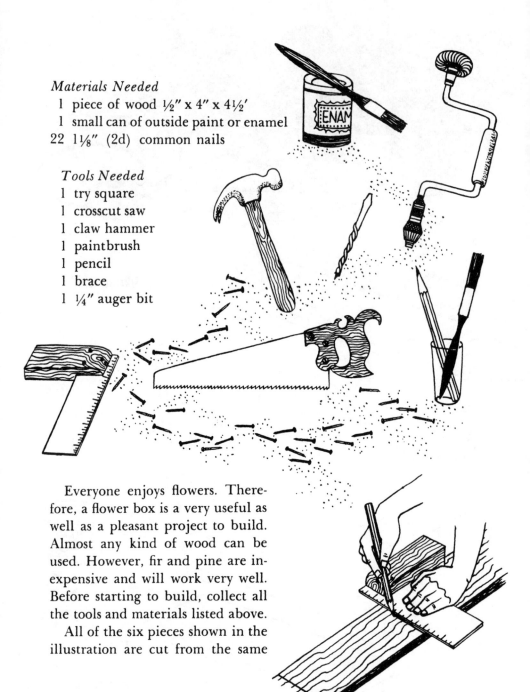

Materials Needed

1 piece of wood $\frac{1}{2}$" x 4" x $4\frac{1}{2}$'
1 small can of outside paint or enamel
22 $1\frac{1}{8}$" (2d) common nails

Tools Needed

1 try square
1 crosscut saw
1 claw hammer
1 paintbrush
1 pencil
1 brace
1 $\frac{1}{4}$" auger bit

Everyone enjoys flowers. Therefore, a flower box is a very useful as well as a pleasant project to build. Almost any kind of wood can be used. However, fir and pine are inexpensive and will work very well. Before starting to build, collect all the tools and materials listed above.

All of the six pieces shown in the illustration are cut from the same board. Make the two sides by measuring off and marking two 10-inch pieces from a good end of your board. Use the square and pencil for drawing lines on the marks, to indicate where you should make your cut. Cut on these lines with a crosscut saw. Saw slowly and carefully when you get to the end of your cut so as not to split the board.

Make the bottom the same way but 3 inches wide and 9 inches long.

Following the same procedure, measure, mark and cut off two 4-inch pieces for the ends. To give the ends shape, measure in $\frac{1}{2}$-inch from each end of the bottom of each end piece. Draw a line from these marks to the nearest top corners of the piece. Cut on all four lines with the crosscut saw.

A false bottom is used to provide drainage. Make this by cutting a piece of wood 9 inches long and $3\frac{1}{8}$ inches wide, the same way you cut the regular bottom. Drainage is provided by drilling

eight ¼-inch holes in this false bottom. Space these holes throughout the false bottom as shown in the drawing.

Fasten the sides to the ends by using three 1⅛-inch common nails at each side. Place the regular bottom in place inside the bottom frame. Use two nails to fasten each of the ends to the bottom. Then nail each side to the bottom with three nails. This will give a tight fit.

Give the false bottom and both the inside and outside of the box two coats of whatever color paint you decided upon. After the paint has dried, place the false bottom in place, fill the box within ¾-inch of the top with good garden soil and you are ready to plant.

STEPS IN SQUARING A BLOCK OF WOOD

Pieces of wood do not always come in the exact width and length that you want them. Usually it is the length that you have to cut. Because of this, detailed directions are given on how to do this for each project in the book. Because, from time to time, it is also necessary to cut a board down in width, specific directions for the entire process are given here in four steps.

1. *Plane one edge straight and square. Use a smooth plane and test with a try square both ways.*

By this we mean plane one edge until it is completely straight lengthwise and crosswise. Test it by holding the back of the blade of a try square on this edge lengthwise and sidewise. If you can see a hollow under the square or if the square rocks, your edge is neither straight nor square and needs to have the high spots planed off.

A plane is one of the best woodwork-

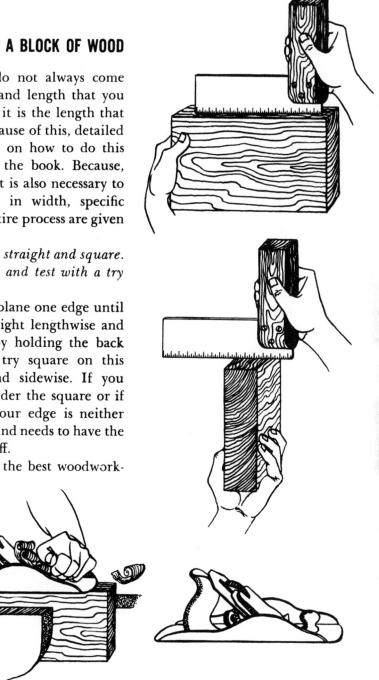

ing tools to use when making edges straight and square. To use a woodworking plane, grasp the front knob with your left hand and the back with your right. Place the front end of the plane on the edge of your board and then push straight across.

2. Measure width desired. Use a marking gauge or ruler and draw a pencil along the line. Saw off excess wood with a rip saw, and plane to the line. Test with a try square both ways.

In this case you measure the width of wood that you need and mark this with a pencil line. Then saw and plane to the line and test this edge.

A marking gauge is a ruler with a point for marking and a stop that is adjusted at the desired measurement. Look at the illustration to see how to hold and use a marking gauge.

A rip saw is used for sawing with the grain. Notice that the teeth form a series of chisels that

FROM THE SIDE

FROM BELOW
RIP SAW TEETH

chisel a groove through the board.

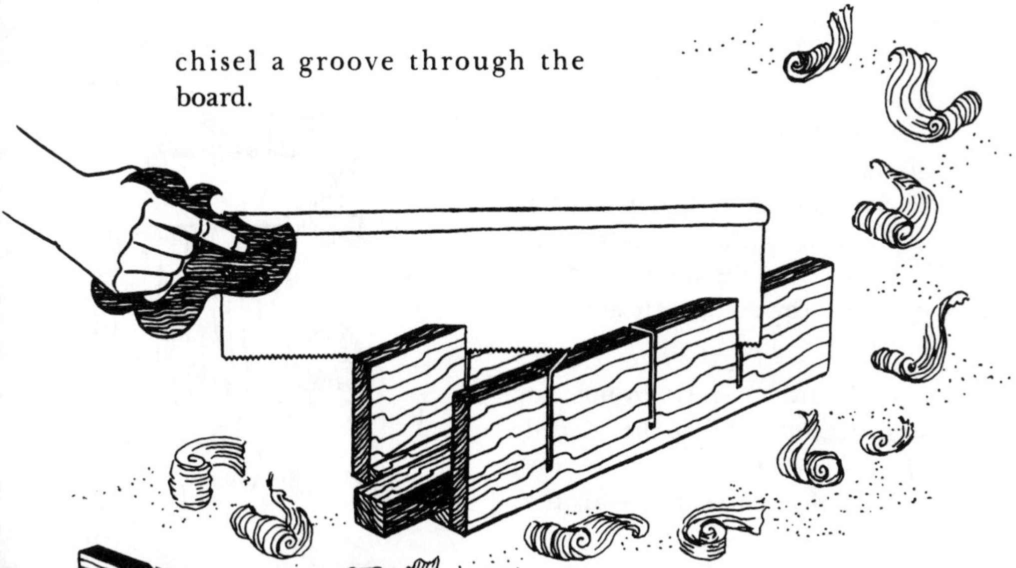

3. *Cut off one end in a mitre box or mark off this end with a try square and cut off with a crosscut saw.*

In this step you square off one end of a board so you have a good starting point from which to measure.

A mitre box is a wooden or metal frame that guides a saw, when a saw cut is being made. The saw cut is so guided that it is always straight and square when you saw through the two middle slots. (To obtain an end with an angle for a "mitred" corner you use the diagonal slots as shown above.)

4. *Measure length desired. Cut off surplus wood in the mitre box or mark this end with a try square and cut off with a crosscut saw.*

In this step the board is measured the correct length and cut off straight and square.

CAUTION: If ends are not cut straight and have to be planed off, be sure to plane from the edge to the center, never all the way across.

STEPS IN WOOD FINISHING

Finishing (or painting) a project is just as important as making the project. These simple directions tell you how to put a nice finish on all of your work.

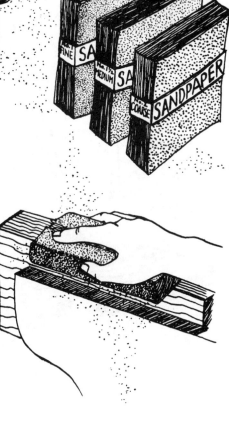

1. Collect all the pieces of the project and check them for accuracy.

2. Sandpaper each piece on all faces, edges, and ends. *Sandpaper with the grain.* Use No. 1½ or No. 2 sandpaper.

3. After the project is assembled, scrape off any excess glue and erase all of the pencil marks.

4. Sandpaper the entire object, with the grain, using No. 1 or 0 (fine) sandpaper.

5. Stir all paint before you start to use

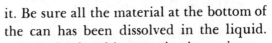

it. Be sure all the material at the bottom of the can has been dissolved in the liquid.

6. Stain the object or give it a prime or basic coat of paint. If you stain, wipe off with a rag. If you paint, let it dry overnight.

7. Shellac the stained work and give the painted work a coat of enamel.

8. Give the object a second coat of either shellac or enamel if this appears to be

necessary, but wait until the first coat is dry.

9. Apply any additional designs or surface decorations that you desire.

10. Put covers on all paint cans and jars. Make sure they are really tight so that air cannot enter and dry up the paint. Store away from fires and warm places.

11. Clean the brushes very carefully. Shellac brushes are cleaned in alcohol. Paint, enamel, and varnish brushes are cleaned in turpentine or paint thinner. All brushes should then be washed with soap and warm water.

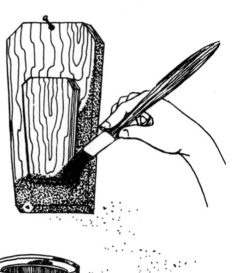